MEDITERRANEAN CULTURE

MEDITERRANEAN CULTURE

BY

JOHN L. MYRES

THE FRAZER LECTURE 1943

CAMBRIDGE
AT THE UNIVERSITY PRESS
1943

CAMBRIDGE
UNIVERSITY PRESS

University Printing House, Cambridge CB2 8BS, United Kingdom

Published in the United States of America by Cambridge University Press, New York

Cambridge University Press is part of the University of Cambridge.

It furthers the University's mission by disseminating knowledge in the pursuit of
education, learning and research at the highest international levels of excellence.

www.cambridge.org
Information on this title: www.cambridge.org/9781107697966

© Cambridge University Press 1943

First published 1943
Re-issued 2014

A catalogue record for this publication is available from the British Library

ISBN 978-1-107-69796-6 Paperback

MEDITERRANEAN CULTURE

AN ESSAY IN GEOGRAPHICAL HISTORY

In the Frazer Lecture of 1937, Henry Balfour distinguished and compared what he described as 'spinners' and 'weavers' in anthropological research; those who supply the substantial well-scrutinized threads of attested fact, and those who will unite these, in the textile process, into a fabric with a pattern, interlacing the 'warp' of facts with the 'weft' of argument. Some of the most eminent of my predecessors have been 'spinners' and 'weavers' as well, like him whom these lectures have commemorated. But in a short hour, so few threads can be added to the warp, so few passes of the weft to the fabric and the pattern, that I propose to stand aside from the loom, and see how that fabric and pattern begin to look, into which any warp or weft of mine may have been interwoven. The fabric and the pattern: but not, I fear, the living colour: not because this is a lecture, not a book; nor because some of the colours have faded everywhere, and in some parts all; but because a more generous humanity and another order of literary art are required for *Psyche's Task*. Yet of institutions and ideas, as of monuments, it is proper to ask, not only *what* they are, and *how* they work, but *when*, and *where*.

It is over fifty years since I first met Frazer, not as the author of the recent *Totemism* or *The Golden Bough*, but as explorer of Greek sites, prospective illustrator of

Pausanias, and sympathetic observer of those beliefs and customs which lay nearest to the soil, in the substructure of Greek society; of those 'little gods', whom Homer and his Olympians might ignore, but whose divinity Hesiod acknowledged, when with Homer he 'made for the Greeks their gods'. In Italy, too, it was one of those 'little gods' in the grove of Aricia who furnished the text for *The Golden Bough*. My present concern, however, is not with gods, great or small, nor with those all-but-superhuman individuals, who like Hesiod's 'heroes' not only had authority and initiative in their lifetime, but continue to direct the course of events by their achievements. Both gods and immortals, in this sense, I take for granted, and turn to the 'little men' to whom both meant so much, the common folk of that *orbis terrarum*, round the Midland Sea, over which Greek freedom spread and Roman authority. What are the permanent features of their mode of life, without which nothing could have been achieved, either by gods or by heroes; upon which have been erected noble superstructures; into which, in evil times, Mediterranean man withdraws to recuperate? What, on the other hand, have been the fortunes of those outland peoples who have been injected into this unique region from elsewhere, deranging that primary culture, and themselves disintegrated by encounter with it?

Orbis Terrarum.

Let us take for granted—together with gods and heroes, and on the other side of the account—the physical and

6

biological circumstances—what Buckle, Marx, and other physicists regarded as 'controls'—which make this geographical region unique as a home for man; not for maintenance only, but for a good life, among those 'external goods' and enjoying them; an aspect of the matter on which Frazer loved to lavish his descriptive skill. But let us note, by way of precaution, how this regime, within a remarkable uniformity, nevertheless varies between oceanic and continental, and how the Mountain-zone, which embraces, or borders, or traverses the main sea-basins, is continuous also eastward into Iran.

Let us take for granted, also, the fundamental trinity-in-unity of its human population; again with the qualification that the men of the Mountain-zone and of the northern and the southern Flatlands remain continuous and relatively homogeneous breeds within their ancient habitats; and that where they have interpenetrated and interbred, the fair-seeming regime of these sea-boards austerely purges and clarifies that *sentina gentium* to a Mediterranean effluent. That regime, moreover, has itself been made austerer by man's agelong devastation, replacing virgin forest by goat-ridden scrub-land or rain-swept rubble and rock. The 'Hill of the Graces', described by Herodotus as 'rich in all kinds of trees', was in the Tarhuna moorland between Misurata and the Wad-el-Kebir. Ovid's *foliis umbrosa Calymne* has no trees left at all. Yet of unexploited Mediterranean we have vivid glimpse in Homer's description, as Odysseus draws inshore to Cyclops-land, and notes, prospector-like, both what it provides, and what it does *not* yet offer, but might be made to yield.

The first human exploitation follows almost as a matter of course, but some aspects of it deserve attention. Materials for such an enquiry as this are the remains of settlements and cultivation terraces, of many periods, plotted on the map; occasional descriptions and allusions in the literatures; and a few significant words, gems and nuggets out of the shingle of speech—*agroikos, apoikia, demokratia.* Greek folk-memory had its 'acorn-eating men', its cannibal Laestrygonians, and wholly pastoral Cyclops-folk, as well as 'milk-eating men without sustenance'; that is, without cereal agriculture. When the gift of grain came to Eleusis, there were only piglets to offer to the Giver. All elements of the Mediterranean, as of the Biblical food-quest, came from the Near East, yet many are but improved strains of what was found wild in Mediterranean lands; so acclimatization was easy. Goats and sheep counted, and still count, for more than either swine or oxen; but all herding is accessory to agriculture, and the meanest of livelihoods. Agriculture, though it has the ox-drawn plough, made (and makes) large use of the hoe. Its basis is threefold, and all three crops—corn, wine, and oil—are the *élite* of the regional plants; the nobler grasses, a deep-rooted deciduous shrub, and a berry-bearing evergreen. Stone-fruit, fig, and mulberry came later out of Anatolia. Confined to the North African coast-oases is a tropical intruder, the date palm. As the Arabs say: 'Put its feet in the river and its head

8

in hell': the Mediterranean has little of either. Yet in one lush cove of eastern Crete palms grow wild.

A mode of life so dependent on the produce of trees is necessarily sedentary. Cultivable land being everywhere limited, the farm, as population outgrew subsistence, was extended uphill by terracing, downhill by reclamation of fen, both at the risk of devastation by rain-spate. But the evil day was only postponed, and perhaps aggravated; the smaller areas suffering most, and the islands worst of all. From Minos to Mussolini, the gods look out over that world, and see it overfull of men; and a robust nature-worship, approved by gods old and new, offers no remedy.

Had either Greek city-state, or Italic *municipium*, or mediaeval Italian city, been a fundamental or essential form, or political *idea*, we might have expected each of them to have made a better struggle for survival; and the fact that each was superseded in its turn challenges the question: *what is*, in contrast with these efflorescences, the cultural root out of which they emerged, and into which their people have relapsed, again and again?

That there has been such abiding type or pattern of community, must have been the discovery of many who know the modern country-side, in Spain, in Italy, in Greece, in Anatolia, in Palestine; above all in Cyprus, Crete, and Sicily; in Sardinia and Corsica, and in the highlands of Atlantic Africa; or who have compared the outlay of a Minoan village, a deserted Moslem site in Crete, and a village of the Aurès or Khoumiria. These

9

likenesses are not casual, nor due to geographical 'controls' over settlements and peoples formerly different; for they recur in detail among the arts and crafts, and the rest of the cultural heritage. In the bazaar of Tripolitan Homs, the hand-made pottery, which has survived alongside Arab *bilbils* and Hellenistic *amphorae*, resembles that of neolithic Cyprus and Malta. The downward tapering columns of Minoan 'palaces' have their prototype in the tree-trunks which are set roots upwards in the Aurès for better lodgment of roof-beams. The Berber women pin their 'Doric chiton' with a fibula on either shoulder, and weave esparto cornbins of the same stature and basket-ornament as their clay skeuomorphs, the Knossian *pithoi*. Whether still within the frame of tribal society, as in North Africa and in Albania, or self-contained where tribal structure has been long disintegrated, these economic units have essentially the same social structure; an association of hereditary groups engaged in the same food-quest, and administered by a more or less formal council of the heads of these groups.

All this gives vivid reality to Aristotle's account of the *kômê* as an economic and social association 'for more than diurnal use', namely to subserve the farmer's year; and he expressly contrasts this, and some peculiar groupings of its members, with the more inclusive aim and end of the *polis*. Concentrating his learning and critical reason on the *polis*, and specifically on its political achievement, he has diverted attention from alternative modes of advancement, some within his own experience, like the federal unions of Western Greece. He studied Carthage, because he ranked it as a *polis*; but he passed by the Numidian kingdom and the queer Libyan societies known to Herodotus, as he passed by the *pagi* and *municipia* of Italy, the Iberian communities described later by Diodorus, and the *nomoi* of Egypt. Even his genuine interest in Macedonian kingship did not extend to the structure of the Macedonian kingdom.

On some Mediterranean coasts, Greek colonies devastated the native communities, and the local principalities in which they were sometimes aggregated—for we hear of 'kings' and other territorial magnates. But though there are examples of perennial resentment and recurrent aggression, the colonists often made friendly agreements for trade and transport. Eventually there seems to have been more or less explicit dependence of tribes and townships on the Greek city for defence; and of the Greek citizens on native cultivators for maintenance: with occasional revolt against oppression, or transference of allegiance to native aggressors, such as the King of Macedon, or the Sabellian peoples of Italy.

In Sicily, the fertile and populous interior was organized by a native leader, taking advantage of feuds between Dorian and Chalcidian cities on the coast to press the claim of 'Sicily for the Sicilians'; and it was remembered against imperial Athens that not only did she intervene between Dorian and Chalcidian states, but supported a Sicel town, Egesta, against its Greek neighbour. Later, the ease with which Rome dominated the island was partly due to the desire of the Sicel communities to be rid of both Greek and Carthaginian parasites; and later again the so-called 'Slave Wars' were dangerous because the 'slaves' not only included native serfs, but had the support of the country-side, and held the Sicel sanctuary and fortress of Enna. In Sardinia and Corsica we know less of the native communities, but enough of their resistance to Rome, to draw similar conclusions. In Spain, the position had been complicated, before the Roman and even the Punic occupation, by Celtic immigration; and in the regions east of Celtic Italy, by Illyrian, Thracian, and earlier movements out of Danubian Europe. But the nearer we come to the north-western limit of Greek speech, the clearer is the evidence for 'unwalled villages'—the Aristotelian *kômê*—within the tribal framework, in classical times. In Roman Caria survived what Strabo calls 'systems of demes' and here a Turkish administrative district with about thirty villages is still called the 'Carian plain' (*kar·ova*). Thucydides describes 'unwalled villages' in Aetolia. From such *kômai* a *polis* was constituted at Mantinea and in Elis in the fifth century, and into them unwanted Mantinea was dissolved in the fourth. In Thales' remedy for federal inefficiency in Ionia, the cities 'were to be inhabited as before, but to rank as if they were *demes*'. Most notable of all, in the immemorial *demes* of Attica we have the social and economic indivisibles into which the tribal *polis* was dissolved by Clisthenes, and out of which the new ten tribes were compiled. It is quite unnecessary to suppose that the new political term *demokratia* was coined for Attic use. It is certainly older than Clisthenes, and goes back, as a term of abuse, to the Homeric contrast of *demos* and *polis*. In the mouth of the 'man-about-town'—*polites, asteios, agoraios*—it meant government by country-cousins—*agroikoi* or at best *demotai*—who had a 'tavern in the town' like the men of Decelea, but little more. Many other Greek city-states are known to have had such substructures, sometimes explicitly described as *demoi* or *kômai*.

It has been necessary to anticipate the study of such relations between primary economic associations, and the political organisms which embody them, in order to establish both their priority and a geographical distribution so wide that they may be accepted as characteristic, and probably ubiquitous, in Mediterranean lands, except where agriculture was impracticable.

Such, then, were the primary associations of sedentary folk, throughout Mediterranean lands; close-knit villages, producing, maintaining, replacing their inhabitants in such mode of life as their surroundings allowed; and governed by the headmen of each tribal group, or ward, which composed them. In the remoter regions, Tunis and Algeria, Balkan lands, Anatolia, and Syria, this is the normal aggregate, and limit of social advancement; into these all higher cultures relapse, where conditions become austere. Even Greek cities occasionally went into liquidation. When Athens became the capital of modern Greece, it was a dilapidated hamlet of this kind, its tiny church, the *monasteraki*, crouching by Hadrian's ruined market and the Turkish mosque. Defensible positions being rare, and water-supply within reach of them even rarer, proximity to the fields is secondary and a matter of degree: in the busiest season and shortest nights men keep their 'feast of tabernacles' in wind-breaks among the corn. Herdsmen, similarly, move with the flocks seasonally between upland and lowland pastures; and this transhumance, like all vestiges of nomadism, stunts economic and social advancement, as may be seen to-day in Sicily and South Italy, Eurafrica, Anatolia, and most of the Mountain-zone. Physical discontinuity of cultivable land obstructs intercourse, and concentrates attention on local affairs and especially on local grievances; for it is the least civilized individuals—upland goatherds, 'wild, seditious, rambling' like their charges—who encounter neighbours like unto themselves on the ridges.

For the satisfaction of needs or desires beyond this traditional and austere routine, men must seek abroad: (1) for maintenance, if that fails them at home—and to this we must return, (2) for material rarities—metals, drugs, amulets, and (3) for needs of the soul, when the 'little gods' are helpless. These external needs the *bazaar* and the *sanctuary* exploit, perennially, without claiming political dominance themselves; though either may become the regional base for dynastic rule—Damascus under Benhadad and Hazael, Palmyra under Zenobia, Jerusalem under Solomon and the Maccabees.

In a region so physically uniform it was necessary to

go far for anything unusual. The generalization of Herodotus, that the most distant lands are richest in rarities, is ingenuous inversion of the fact that only rare and desirable things, 'gold, frankincense, and myrrh', are worth transmitting far. This, however, is a matter of degree; throughout the Mediterranean world, there were (and are) communities—perhaps more numerous, formerly, than we know—which served an essentially economic function, to facilitate exchange of commodities; some for local convenience only, like the *suk*-villages of North Africa, others as stages along through-routes, but the more important at forks and crossings. The Romans called such a place simply a *forum*, 'market', the Greeks an *agora* or *kômopolis*, because whatever their size and structure, their function seemed to be economic, not political. We may perhaps be content to call them 'bazaar' or 'bazaar-city', with Rostovtseff's 'caravan-city' as a major species. On the scale of this diagrammatic analysis, it is not necessary to separate productive from distributive centres, or industry from trade; for it matters not to the customer whether what he buys is produced a hundred miles away, or next door. Sardis, Athens, Corinth, like Manchester and Johannesburg, became great 'bazaars' because they had a commodity of their own to sell. Their prosperity and security—for some became very rich—depended on the worldly wisdom of their merchants, a close guild with wide connexions, to judge when to resist, when to compromise or submit; their own interests, security and revenue, being those of any reasonable 'rule of force'. Examples are the Phoenician cities: Carthage, Tarentum, and Massilia; Cordova, Venice, Genoa and Pisa, later. The Romans, whose own villages on the seven hills looked down over a *forum* in their midst, made abundant use of *fora* as administrative centres, in east and west alike.

What the bazaar-city provided for material needs, the 'sanctuary-city' offered for those of the spirit. The Greek *hierapolis*—'holy city'—is explicit, and when Greeks came to know Jerusalem, they gave it a punning translation *Hierosolyma*. 'Hither the tribes go up' from the countryside, but stricken souls, one by one, make pilgrimage (*peregrinatio*) from afar, to consult seer or shrine: I have heard an oracle distinguished from prophet and from sanctuary, as the conjunction of an uncanny place and a canny person. Some of the greater sanctuaries illustrate also those cults of the dead and that belief in immortality to which Frazer devoted so much study; which Herodotus noted as characteristic of the Libyans; and of which the monuments are ubiquitous from Kairwan to Compostella. Some of them, like Jerusalem, were old tribal fortresses; others, like Ancyra and Pessinus, old bazaars. All alike dispensed 'the peace of God which passeth understanding', accumulated wealth for service rendered, and were governed by the spiritual household of the deity. After Alexander's time, many an old *Hierapolis* became a chartered city-state. Mecca is a supreme instance of a sanctuary-city which was also a bazaar-city; Siwa, Jerabub, Kairwan have been preserved, like Mecca, by

Moslem canonization. In Greek lands the sanctuaries were kept out of worldly mischief by Greek commonsense, Delphi less successfully than smaller places. Delos, after its one political adventure, became rich as a bazaar; Ephesus as an administrative centre. In the west we need only note Sicilian Palice, Latin Aricia, and Gaulish Tolosa.

With the 'sanctuaries', as with the 'bazaars', a despot had little difficulty in coming to terms. Theocracy needs all the sanctions it can obtain: a sanctuary needs peace, for its pilgrims as well as its estates; and if peace could not quite be had for a blessing, a little gold balanced the account. Persian dealings with Jerusalem illustrate ambiguous utterances of Greek oracles where Persia was concerned.

Neither the 'bazaar' nor the 'sanctuary', however, affected the life history of the primary economic association. Each ministered to the needs of individuals, without deranging or enhancing the well-being of the group. To exploit either of them, as a means to power over men's bodies or souls, is an abuse: that is what distinguishes every monopoly and every church from any 'rule of force'. At most they stimulated production or industry, to supply themselves or their clients; they had too much to gain from the world as it was, to attempt changes, economic or political.

Now as long as circumstances and societies remain in equilibrium, there can be no economic, no political, very rarely any moral or intellectual change. Hence the survival of so many primitive Mediterranean people—rather than peoples—in Eurafrica, in Balkan lands, in Anatolia, and (perhaps most notable of all) in Crete and the smaller Aegean islands. And we should note that even in the most advanced and (up to a certain point) progressive cultures of the Mediterranean the confessed goal was statical equilibrium; to 'hand on undiminished' what you have received in trust. In a hard wild world the risks of acquisition—*pleonexia* the Greeks called it—were too great. Nature, the Gods, the Order of the World, were against the man who did not know his place, which—as Delphi taught—meant also knowing himself.

But there was also the risk of having too little, and for this the Gods, great or small, knew no remedy. Though the calamity of dearth usually fell on all alike over a wide area, occasional local disasters drove men to despair and to violence. All agriculture spreads at the expense of hunting-grounds, and residual hunters, reinforced by destitute peasants, can turn the tables on more fortunate villages. Aristotle reckons brigandage, like piracy, in his survey of livelihoods; and in modern regions and phases of misery men still 'go to the hills', like Greek *klephts* a century ago, and Greek and Serb peasants to-day.

In North Africa, otherwise such a museum of primary societies, there are two unsolved problems. One is the origin, so far from the dynastic regimes of the Near East, but so closely resembling them, of the kingdoms of Numidia and Mauretania; of which the first figures already in the foundation-legend of Carthage, and the second looms up beyond Numidia in the second and first centuries B.C. The other is the origin of the famous Barbary horse, ancestor of our thoroughbred stock, as well as of the noblest Arab breed, but zoologically distinct from the wild horses of Asia. To the memory of Sir William Ridgeway, to whom I have owed much, I dedicate the suggestion that the two problems are connected, if not one and the same; that it was the Barbary horse—for which the great intermont plains of Atlas were well suited—that made possible the domination of wide regions by a few princely families, and later the conquest of both Atlantic Africa and Spain by Carthage; and that the absence of early reference to horse-using tribes in North Africa would be explained if Libya, whatever its wealth in indigenous horses, had its knowledge of their use in war from the same source and at the same period as Egypt, namely from Western Asia between the nineteenth and the sixteenth century B.C. Certainly Libyan tribes had horses and four-horse cars in the fifth century, and Carthage used horses in war; but it is not clear that the Libyan invaders of Egypt in the thirteenth century had either chariots or cavalry. Those later horse-using dynasties are significant here, because they are the only large political superstructures which at first sight seem to be indigenous in the Mediterranean.

Other superstructures have been of various kinds— Minoan 'palaces', Greek and Phoenician 'city-states', theocratic despotisms and other 'rules of force' (in Greek, *dynasteiai*), and in mediaeval times, dynasties without pretext of theocratic sanction. But before examining

these, even in briefest outline, there is another characteristic of Mediterranean life to be taken into account.

The Midland Sea

Hitherto Mediterranean culture has been presented
statically, as occupying cultivable portions of an *orbis
terrarum* around a central sea. It was only by anticipation
that account was taken of oversea settlements. But that
is only one aspect of the matter. 'Two Voices are there'—
let us listen now to that of the sea.

The distribution of racial types and primary industries
shows that seafaring is immemorial in Mediterranean
culture. It is also fundamental. Indeed it has been given
as differentia between Ancient East and Mediterranean,
that whereas along the great rivers higher cultures emerged
with irrigation (the redistribution of flowing water over
the land), around the Midland Sea navigation redistributed
land and people alike over the static surface of the water;
every timber-raft and ship proclaiming itself, by its ensign,
to be a detached migratory portion of its land of origin.
Of that home-land its crew are deemed inhabitants, they
are bound by its customs, they retain its language and
culture wherever they go. Hence the contrast between
Demolin's thesis: '*comment la route crée le type social*', and
the way of a ship in the sea, which suffers no change
as it leaves no trail; nor do its cargoes or its passengers.

Of this new frictionless, almost effortless, transport in
bulk, between regions of complementary resources, the
Mediterranean is first and original home, though with

perhaps less priority over the Baltic than has been sup-posed, and certainly some debt to the Nile, though the contrast between Egyptian river craft and seagoing vessels is perplexing. Within the Mediterranean the Aegean archipelago was a primeval sailor's paradise, its ensign-bearing vessels quite early in the bronze age testifying to traffic between independent states.

But there are three ways in which a ship may be used. It may transfer people to new homes coastwise, as popula-tion grows, distributing their mode of life, their institu-tions, and their ideas. That leads to *colonization*, as we have seen. It may distribute and exchange commodities, caravan-like, domesticating the steady currents of a tide-less sea, its daily land-and-sea breezes, and its seasonal trade-winds, as Egypt and Babylonia had harnessed their rivers for transport, and the desert folk their camels. That leads to *commerce*, of the Mediterranean and eventually of the oceanic type. But it is possible also to cut the ship adrift from its home-port, without registering it in another; to make of it the crew's home and castle; to go 'roving' on the high seas, like a cattle-riever out of the hills, or an Ishmaelite out of the desert. That leads to *piracy*, as we shall see; and piracy became as charac-teristic a feature of Mediterranean culture as either com-merce or colonization.

Around the Western Mediterranean and in its islands, many varieties of an ancient and fundamentally uniform culture demonstrate, by their maritime distribution, early sea-traffic, which can be roughly dated by Aegean contacts to the third and second thousand years B.C. All seem to be the work of adventurers from the eastern basin—'prospectors' as they have been called—of distinct breed but uncertain origin, and little subsequent intercourse with their home-land. Their settlements in Sardinia are heavily fortified—maybe against each other; the Maltese monuments are certainly sanctuaries, but without eastward votaries; and this abrupt limit eastward makes more remarkable the wide westward expansion of this 'megalithic' culture along the Atlantic coast of Europe. The significance of these western cultures is as evidence of indigenous character and ability which somehow failed to achieve much, and had relapsed before the colonial age of Greece.

Of the Minoan regime we begin to know enough to estimate its dateable advent, its Egyptian affinities, its later acceptance of Anatolian and Babylonian elements—especially its adaptation of hieroglyphic symbols to clay tablet technique in its pre-cuneiform phase—and its later remodelling into highly centralized 'Palace' organizations, the prototype of which is in the open village of Gournià. The mainland centres seem to me essentially intrusive colonial exploitations. Though they achieved independence, and outgrew the old establishments in Crete, their scripts came specifically from 'palatial' Knossos, and they interfered little with the primary communities even of their own neighbourhood, except perhaps in Attica.

Greek colonization needs further analysis, because the antecedents of Greek colonists were different, and in some respects unique. Whatever their landward origin, the 'divine-born' dynasties, of Homeric folk-memory, like their Phrygian counterparts from Thrace to Lycia, were dynasties and little more. Beyond their sea-front lay other dynasties, and outland; they raided, but did not need to settle, till some of them were expelled. The Homeric *polis* is nothing but a fortress, the *demos* nothing but the country-side in explicit serfdom to the 'divine-born'; and that social gulf both contributed to their utter collapse, and assured the remarkable continuity, archaeologically attested, between the nature-worship of the bronze age, and the 'little gods' of the Hellenic country-side.

In the Hellenic city-states what we chiefly note in this connexion is their geographical distribution. Within their Aegean cradle-land, they are rare and rickety in Thessaly; grouped in regional rather than tribal confederations throughout Central Greece; almost absent from the North-West—where alone Greek colonies, of the tied Corinthian type, stand within a Greek-speaking region; sparse and belated in Elis and Arcadia; deformed by race-feud in Argolis and the Isthmus-cities, and in Boeotia; mature, on the other hand, in the island world, from Aegina and Euboea to the foreshore of Asia; and achieving full stature and integrity in Attica alone, on a scale which permits us to compare the political *polis* with its economic and social constituents, the *demes*; whereas in Laconia, though there were many *demes*, the great majority remained outside the *polis*.

But the *polis*, though a superb instrument for 'living well' in its cradle-land, only found its full utility when a crisis of congestion compelled exodus oversea; and then the marked uniformity of maritime conditions made it easy to find a 'home-away-from-home'. Here we reach one of the many contradictions which make things Greek hard to understand—between an ideal of statical balance, inherent in the primary economy and explicit in Greek political theory, and its opposite, the realization of a new kind of life worth living for politically minded men, a life of adventure and exploitation.

It is only in the New World, and in the crucial instance of the United States, that what is there called the 'frontier' has been at all fully explored by historians. But it is of general applicability; a historical conception—combining a geographical predicament, an economic impulse, and something far more than economic, a release from constraint; *freedom*, in the absolute and literal sense, engendering not an outlook only but an individual type. The Homeric portrait of the Phoenician 'go-getter' has its pendant in that of Odysseus himself—had there not been Penelope and Telemachus in Ithaca; his way with the Cyclops recalls the 'fire-water' of a buccaneer. The frontiersman's world, 'so full of a number of things', is a good world, but will be so much better and fuller, when he and other free men have applied to it their freedom and initiative. What a tragedy, that this was the outlook of the Persians too! It is also apparently limitless. Did not the *Argo* sail the western main and return by the

'Blue Rocks'? The 'ships of Tarshish', with their three-years' round-trip, were the precursors of Necho's venturers and of Scylax. There then is the solution of our paradox. In Greece, men who dreaded the limitless (*apeiron*) sat at home and meditated on it.

It is significant that Greek colonization, comparable in intensity, for about two centuries, with Malayan and with British, followed the main lines of Minoan expansion, and outran it. For those who participated, what 'plantations' were in modern Europe, and the 'frontier' in the New England oversea, is represented by this Greek notion of the 'home-away-from-home', with scope for that aggressive independent austere individualism, which combines political equality with social fraternity and economic liberty, and makes nineteenth-century California redolent of sixth-century Ionia. The new technique of seafaring needed more than the mentality of the *kômê*, or even of the fishing village. And what began with escape seaward bred a habit of mind and endeavour, which outranged the seaways. Though the first Greek *apoikiai* did not usually pass the coastline, yet Cyrene lay twelve miles from its port, and two thousand feet above it; and Philippopolis was the working model for Alexandria-Eschate.

To the wider achievements of seaborne traffic the Phoenician cities contributed as much as they did, because they were also caravan terminals, using the 'ship of the desert'—and indeed the ship may no less be described as the 'camel of the sea', in its immense load-capacity, its terminal intake of water and stores, its ability to keep a course without land-marks, the cultural aloofness of its managers from the detail of other men's lives. It is the same double function, as ports and caravan-terminals, that characterizes the Punic cities, and so nearly made it possible for Carthage—at first a mirror-image of Tyre—to come to an agreement with Rome. But Carthage had exploited the Barbary horse, for use as well as for profit; and was tempted into land-empire. There are, however, three coasts to the Western Mediterranean. It was Hamilcar's vow of vengeance for Sicily and Sardinia, that drove him into Iberia, and Rome's conquest of Iberia that sealed the fate of Carthage.

Punic cities, however, were probably more like Greek *apoikiai* than their rivals admitted, and were certainly of similar origin, in the outflow of narrow home-lands, constrained moreover by Assyrian aggression about 850 B.C., to found Carthage, and by Babylonian after 600 B.C., to exploit Sicily and Sardinia. Certainly in Carthage the constitution was that of a Phoenician city.

The Tyrrhenian migration, too, seems to have resulted from dearth and disorder at home. But without sea-power it could not have wandered far; and it may have swept westward some 'sea-raiders' and unwanted mercenaries. From their names, Tyrrhenia, Sicilia, and Sardinia loom up as the 'blessed isles' of Tursha, Shakalsha, and Shardana; and in Etruscan *lucumones*, with their blood-sports, we recognize the 'lords of the Philistines' out of the Book of Judges, 'sea-raiders' who had burned their boats and cut their way into unfriendly backwood. But of the dominant ideas in Punic and Tyrrhenian minds, we have only hostile depreciation. It is not from the Spanish buccaneers that we learn the character of Elizabethan Englishmen.

All these enterprises are brought together at this point, to illustrate the profound disorganization of early modes of life in the Mediterranean by men with 'frontier' outlook, and ships with which to give effect to it. At a later stage Arab seafaring followed the same course, both in these waters and east of Suez, their technical invention of the 'lateen' sail giving them superior ease of manœuvre. No one who has seen a mounted Arab make horse or camel move rapidly *sideways* need wonder that desert-bred man first made a ship sail up-wind.

So rapidly was this 'frontier' phase achieved, that most of the regions fit for colonization were already occupied, before Persian conquest displaced other swarms of refugees, and Sparta made half-hearted attempts to settle them in Libya and in Western Sicily. But already, before the Persians came, the tide was turning, and Greek adventurers were finding new outlets, in 'pacific penetration' of Lydia and Egypt, and less pacific employment as mercenaries of Babylonian and of Saite kings. In the west there was scramble and clash, Greek against Carthaginian and Etruscan. The attempts of half-Hellenized natives to meet Greek immigrants with their own weapons, at Olynthus, Mylasa, Egesta, Barca—perhaps at Capua— were rare and not successful enough to be repeated.

By 'their own weapons' I mean specifically here the political instrument which made Greek colonization possible and so permanent as it was. When English adventurers landed on a New England beach, they knew exactly, almost instinctively, what to do next. They called a town's-meeting and elected a mayor and a sheriff. The 'borough' was in their very blood, not 'for maintaining life' merely, but for living as good a life as Englishmen knew how. So too in a Greek 'home-away-from-home'. Delphi provided indeed an *oikistes*, one of those men 'whom the Muses love', as Hesiod says, and Calliope most of all; 'with gentle speech' getting things done 'quietly and easily'; 'getting men together' as Aristotle puts it, and so conferring on them 'the greatest blessings'. But those others were city-born *politai*; 'conformity and initiative in turn' were in their blood; tribes and phratries, councillors and justices crystallized out from the fluid 'polity', by harmonic law of their breeding. For these were 'political animals', a new species of humanity, evolved in the dark 'iron' age between the Homeric and the colonial; and competent to employ the old device of navigation in this new 'frontier' spirit.

But however well bred to 'keep house together' English and Spanish settlers in the New World may have been—and partly because their political notions were so ingrained—neither they nor the Greek 'homes-away-from-home' had any place at their fireside, still less at the town's-meeting, for natives. Here and there a Thracian or Libyan strain distinguished a *voortrekker* family, like

Iroquois or Aztec blood among other frontiersmen. But where there was greater laxity, it was deeply resented. The hyphenated Megara-Hyblaea was a byword, to be remembered when men speak of Greek indifference to 'colour-bar'. Gelo had no use for what we call 'mean whites'. The 'brotherhood of man' was proclaimed in Greek science by Eratosthenes from Cyrene, where some Greeks were black, and in philosophy by Zeno of Citium, a Phoenician. Even in Larisa, which had roused the mirth of Gorgias from Leontini, only Thessalians could apply for citizenship. Here, at first encounter, is a great gulf fixed between the 'political animal' and the 'lesser breeds without the Law'. Social fraternity; economic liberty, perhaps; but political equality, *no*! Thus the pioneer cities of the Mediterranean remained set like gems in base metal. They might, and did, benefit the native communities, not without reward, and exploit them without redress, but they *could* not incorporate them. Only in the miracle wrought by Demonax at Cyrene did one of his three tribes consist of 'Libyan neighbours'. We must reserve till later the Roman solution of this problem, which does not depend on sea-transport at all.

Commerce, seaborne like the colonists, was not only essential to the well-being of oversea settlements, but revolutionized the economy of production at both ends. Many of the colonies were exploiting regions of very different resources from those of the 'old country'; in particular, outside the rugged Mountain-zone, of which the Aegean is a half-submerged section, were lands not only suited to corn-growing, on a prairie scale, but unsuited to olives and unplanted as yet with vines. Ancient oil-presses around Miletus, and the text-book example of Solon's Athens, like Herodotus' distinction between 'corn for food' and 'corn for sale' in Scythia, illustrate the specialization that ensued; as the rarity of famine during the great age of Greece shows the relative security of the corn-supply, compared with that of the Near East, which is land-borne. This comprehensive trade system enabled Hellenism to maintain a coherent system of ideas, as well as a common standard of the arts of life. When Alexandrian scholars set about a definitive edition of Homer, the 'city-texts' from far and near were among their principal sources. Conversely, though Phoenician culture remained restricted and aloof in essentials, the material remains of Carthage show how much was borrowed, albeit clumsily, from the arts and industries of Greek Sicily.

Industry and the arts migrated too. As men frequent bazaars and sanctuaries for what these supply, so with easier access all higher skill finds its reward in distant markets nearer to the raw material or to the customer; Homer and Arion, Democedes the physician, Herodotus and Anaxagoras, no less than Demaratus of Corinth in Tarquin's Rome. Some communities are nurseries of craftsmen: to speak only of the small islands, Amorgos and Casos breed masons and navvies, and Siphnos, cooks; or have favourite 'homes-away-from-home', sponge-fishers from Calymnos in Florida and the Bahamas, from

Symi in the Argentine, from Castellorizo in Australian Albany. But most of this movement is individual and promiscuous. Slave-trade in the Mediterranean was necessarily sea-trade—Delos is a flagrant instance—but with the mechanism of industry still simple, and all transport costly, other human cargo, adventurers, traders, and artisans, have infiltrated the loose structure of great communities, ancient and modern. Modern intercourse has intensified this dispersal (*diaspora*) but in the Hellenistic world and the Roman Empire it was widespread; and this fluidity of the producers created a new political gulf between a home-bred political class, and an immigrant economic, for which Rome was the first to find a remedy. Like the Jews, though not with their fanatical devotion to their local congregation (*synagogé*), other Mediterranean immigrants cohere socially in their 'homes-away-from home', without as a rule carrying national aspirations into local politics. In modern states they remain 'on deposit', as it were, or 'at call' for their homeland's needs, and are liberal in support of kinsmen and institutions there. If they are passengers in the ship of state, they are at all events not mutinous.

These resident aliens deserve attention, because in all periods of material prosperity their numbers have increased, and in periods of adversity their lack of political security makes them the earliest sufferers economically. The ever-present risk of overpopulation makes this means of adjustment between economic foundation and political superstructure significant. The Greek city-states left the problem unsolved. Of all Mediterranean peoples the Romans came nearest to a remedy.

It was the good fortune of the Romans that their first external dealings were with primary communities of kindred stock, large enough, and exposed to dangers like enough to their own, to permit the political experiment of voluntary incorporation, which Athens so narrowly missed. Solon had encouraged industrial immigrants; Clisthenes reformulated the twofold test of residence and good-fellowship; and this incorporation might have been progressive; perhaps it was intended to be so. But at that point the narrower loyalties prevailed, on both sides of the bargain; Herodotus of Halicarnassus was passed on to Thurii. The solution attributed by him to Thales for an Ionian league was never achieved in the Delian, and only momentarily and partially in the Chalcidic.

To some of its Greek admirers, early Rome seemed 'a most Hellenic city'; but economic accident made it also a bazaar-city, unique in its reception of others beside Latin neighbours. Greek and other alien industrials, attracted under Etruscan rule, became indispensable to the Republic, and their incorporation was achieved, not indeed forthright as at Athens, but by two centuries of characteristic fictions and political compromise. And during those centuries also Rome's nearer 'allies', and earlier enemies, exchanged autonomy for graduated citizenship; municipal careers rewarding political ability with access to full citizenship and so, by popular selection, to Roman magistracy. The two procedures supplement and implement each other. That municipal system was the first—after Clisthenes—to link primary communities organically with a political superstructure. Extended to Celtic townships in the Po valley, and to other native populations from Britain to provincial Africa, it made Rome the capital of the western Mediterranean in a more intimate sense than in the eastern, where, once again, local urban loyalties were less compatible. In the modern Mediterranean, what is significant is the rebirth of this Roman combination of transmarine political citizenship with municipal autonomy in French Africa, and the failure of the Italians to learn from it.

That Roman practice of linking primary associations with civil and eventually with provincial government brings to light many survivals of old economic groupings which passed unnoticed so long as the political relations which mattered were with a dynasty or a city-state. Only occasionally had even sanctuary-states like Pessinus or Jerusalem come into the picture. For Romans, however, and probably for others, the formal 'migration' of the Great Mother from Pessinus to Rome was symbolic, as that of Juno from Veii had been. It was a pathetic gesture, on the Arch of Titus, that depicted Jehovah's 'mercy seat' in transit. This is the significance of the numerous 'communes' (*koina*), composed like the *fora* (p. 15) of villages or small towns united by neighbourhood and productivity round a bazaar or a sanctuary. The frequency of sanctuary-centres is illustrated by the cult-statues on their coins. Within these *koina* the old economic life could (and did) go on, undisturbed except by general causes such as war, famine, or economic distress. Their frequency is apparent again when an episcopal diocese coincides with an administrative district; new 'church' replacing old 'sanctuary'.

Rome thus achieved, what the Greek city-state had foregone, a method by which the primary societies were literally incorporated, like cells in an organic body, and shared its political life as it shared their productivity. We have still to ask why this achievement was not more complete and permanent, and we return for at least a partial answer to the seaways.

Piracy has already been noted as an alternative use of the sea and of ships. Aristotle classes it with brigandage, as a mode of subsistence, but he does not note its significance as an abuse of sea-transport. The Greek words are instructive, as usual. The word *laos* (*leôs*) denotes an organized band with common purpose and leader; and the verb *leïzein* means to let loose such a *laos* on the coast or the country-side; as *populari* in Latin means to let loose a *populus* of armed men. A *leïstês*, then, is a member of such a band or crew; and his other Greek name, which has passed into Latin as *pirata*, characterizes him as always 'trying it on' with unsuspecting people. But 'once bitten, twice shy'. During the last war, when it was necessary, in default of aircraft, to select observation-posts against submarines on Aegean lines of communication, the local names for prominent peaks, *vigla, merovigli, episkopí*, were an unfailing guide; for the older islanders remembered the watchmen, set here day and night to look for pirates, some of the last of whom sacked Chalki Island in the summer of 1893. So endemic is piracy in these waters.

The pirate on a small scale need not come ashore at all, except professionally, or on an unfrequented coast to rest or refit: he victuals and finances himself from his victims. But if he has loot or captives to sell, he may risk a tolerant reception; he may hold a port or an island to ransom; he may have somewhere a Treasure Island, or cove or cave, where he deposits his hoard. His climax is dominion over a larger island like Crete; or of a defensible stretch of coast like Cilicia, Tripoli, Algiers, or the Riff. A famous lair in Astypalaea Island, in mid-Aegean, cannot have been called *Maltezana* till the Knights of the Hospital had withdrawn from Rhodes to Malta. Astypalaea had been one of the outposts of Rhodes, but what were *Maltezi* doing there now? Early in the last century it was the lair of a famous pirate, said to be buried there; and it has proved its utility in the last war and in this.

For the pirate games of 'hide-and-seek' and 'catch-as-catch-can', the Mediterranean and (above all) the Aegean are peculiarly suited. Hence the long succession of 'sea-powers' on which honest seamen have had to rely, so unsuccessfully. Of Minos, 'first of human descent' among these, it was remembered how he 'expelled the Carians from the islands'. Thucydides attributes Hellenic expansion to his successors; of whom the anonymous *List of Sea-powers* enumerates no less than sixteen between the days of Priam and of Xerxes. Eight of them were Greek cities; only one was Phoenician; and one, if correctly recorded, was itself piratical. His enemies deemed Polycrates a pirate too. But all of whom we know anything present the same paradox; that in a world of sovereign and more or less equipotent states, efficient co-operation, even in defence, presumes some surrender of autonomy. It is equally futile to have hegemony without a league, and a league without hegemony. Early services of Athens and of the Delian League were the expulsion of Pelasgian pirates from Lemnos, and of the Dolopes from Scyros, for the general good, or by mandate. With so many nooks and obstacles, a single privateer can do quite extravagant damage; and with so few arsenals and sources of naval supplies, the cost of sea-power has been extravagant also. Athens depended for timber on Thrace-ward backwoods, Rome for crews on 'naval allies', and Turks and Arabs on renegades and galley-slaves. Moreover, to keep seaways safe needs, not great sea-fights, but ceaseless patrol, and that means morale in all ranks, and most of all at the top. Here Rhodes has a better record than Rome, which built highways instead of naval bases.

The long nightmare of mediaeval piracy has left its mark on the demography as well as on the nomenclature. All the smaller communities retreated from the coast to hilltops and headlands—as Thucydides describes in early Greek times—and the larger were heavily fortified. From the *kastro* the peasantry still go forth to their work until the evening. In straggling islands like Cos or Amorgos,

or a long promontory like Cnidus, there has been seg-
mentation into two or more strong points. Only slowly,
as the menace ceased, the *kastro* has spilled its white
houses down the port-way. In Calymnos, it was only
in 1821 that the first houses were built on the strand;
in Scyros, Seriphos, Telos, and Astypalaea there were
hardly a dozen houses at the *scala* till the present century;
and at Samos the growth of tonnage has brought the new
scala into a different bay from the old town. In Algeria,
Sicily, South Italy, and the Riviera it has been the same.

Traced to its Viking origin the Norman kingdom of
Apulia and Sicily was a gigantic adventure of this kind.
It profoundly troubled the waters of the Mediterranean;
it left great monuments in the strategical bases of its sea-
power; but the 'strong man armed' brought upon himself a stronger; like earlier pirate states, Norman adventurers flourished only till neighbouring governments—
like political parties in republican Rome—laid aside their
quarrels for a moment to put an end to the nuisance.
The 'pirate war' of Pompeius lasted sixty days, and left
the survivors boatless and innocuous on their Cilician
farms. For the pirate at home, as at Penzance, is but a
poor orphan, who has never had a chance.

The Norman adventurers learned much from their
Byzantine and arch-pirate admirals, and showed what
was possible, from productive bases, in a Mediterranean
without effective sea-power. Venice, Genoa and Pisa used
the same methods in more respectable causes, the despatch
of pilgrims and crusaders, and in breaking Byzantine

monopoly of luxury-trade. The Crusaders needed only safe-conduct of land forces on an errand not of this world, the rescue of a 'holy place', and struck a bargain with the sea-powers of the time. Their territorial gains were therefore piracy like that of the Normans, and in this Crete and Cyprus played the same unwilling part as Sicily. Their retreat they covered with a sea-power of their own, the Knights of the Hospital, an experiment in 'united nations' and 'freedom of the seas' for pilgrims and traders, exposed to all the risks of such benevolence. Outliving that career, and the Italian sea-powers that had guarded their communications and shared their profits, and ejected from Rhodes by Ottoman sea-power, they failed, perhaps fortunately, to make of Tripoli or of Malta what the Normans had made of Palermo.

Different in degree, rather than in kind, are the successive incursions of sea-borne adventurers and traders from the continent or beyond the Straits. Aragon and Anjou, and later Spain and France, made the most of both worlds, Mediterranean and continental. English and Dutch abode in their ships, the Dutch acquiring no territory, the English only to protect their traders and to plant warehouses ashore. Without access by sea, none of these had any interest in Mediterranean industry or trade, nor in supporting insolvent dynasties, as England and France had done; with access for their fleets as well as their merchantmen, both states have pressed economic intervention far, and for political as well as economic ends; the Midland Sea has thus become a deep gulf of the

38

Atlantic, as the Red Sea had long been of the Indian Ocean. And with the Suez Canal, freedom of seaways acquired a new meaning, as it had, long before, when Varangian ships appeared north of the Bosporus.

This examination of sea-power abused is prompted by the Mediterranean's peculiar facilities for such abuse. But economically and politically it makes no difference, whether the pirate's base is within the Mediterranean or beyond it, any more than whether it is within or beyond the Aegean; nor whether it is Treasure Island or a bandit's cave in the hills—or beyond them. All alike are a 'rule of force', reaping where they have not sown.

All higher forms of political structure within the Mediterranean world have tested, rather than demonstrated, the competence of Mediterranean peoples for self-government, and their ability to give effect to their own political ideas. Principal hindrances have been the great size of the Hellenistic and the Roman world, the wide intervals between its political centres, and the close exclusive incorporation of its cities. This may be a permanent disability of Mediterranean lands, resulting from physical structure; but an obstacle only obstructs till it is surmounted, as mere size has been by mechanical transport. Even where urban centres were most numerous, in peninsular Greece and Western Anatolia, the physical barriers between them were rarely considered, except by the Persians, as problems for engineers. Roman roads, like the Persian postal service, were strategical, for rapid transference of armed forces, or of orders to them. If they touched cities, it was for rest and refreshment, not for intercourse.

Greek colonization, and Roman municipal government—each an essentially home-bred achievement, however related ultimately, like Persian achievement, to Indo-European sources—superimposed uniformities of higher culture, and a cosmopolitan tolerance, on all but the most inaccessible haunts of primitive tribes. But the strength of both was in urban aggregates. Neither appreciably benefited the country-side except by providing consumers for produce, on terms which in effect were servile. The contrast between town and country grew, and is illustrated by the Christian use of *paganus* 'villager' for an adherent of the old cults. Barbarian invasion replaced what remained of indigenous peasantry by un-acclimatized aliens. As foresight and sea-power diminished, local famines, sometimes widespread, loosened the foundations of urban culture, and strained its communications. That gulf between city and peasantry, which began with sea-borne colonization, was widened by sea-borne commerce and aggravated by piracy, and has become an enduring fact of Mediterranean life. That is why the essential dependence of this culture in every phase on its primary economy has been emphasized here throughout.

In what has been said hitherto, Mediterranean lands have been presented as an *orbis terrarum*, a garland of regions encircling a multiple sea-basin which connects them more than it separates. This may be their primary significance, but it is not the whole, as Alexander and the Romans found; and our own experience is the same. The Mediterranean is an inter-continental sea. Its shores have three main backgrounds, geographically reservoirs of the three main sources of its human population; the Eurasian flatland, the Arabian and African flatlands, and the Mountain-zone.

On the impact of European peoples on Mediterranean lands, a few general observations must suffice. Out of the Mountain-zone itself could descend only mountain-folk, forced by exceptional cold or wet, in small groups with their own close structure and specific mode of life; early lake-dwellers into Northern Italy, mediaeval Albanians into Greece; they have been easily absorbed, and had little culture to transmit. All other intruders, whether out of Europe or from elsewhere, have been no less pastoral, but also originally nomad, with the nomad-pastoral outlook on nature as something to be browsed but not altered, and on other breeds of men as cattle to be domesticated and exploited.

Though all European invaders passed through the purgatory, more or less prolonged, of transit through the Mountain-zone, with sedentary interludes in its forest glades, their close tribal grouping conserved the nomad economy of which the words *pecunia* and *tokos* are characteristic; but once acclimatized and sedentary, there was little but their tribal structure to distinguish their settlements—*vicus* and *oikos*—from the primary Mediterranean societies. Larger *gentes* and *nationes* remained coherent enough to control the distribution of dialects and languages, and to supply a morphological prototype for the city-state and the townships of Italy. But it is of the essence of the *polis* that it transcended the bond of kinship; and Latin Rome included Sabines and Etruscans already under its kings.

In the early West, for phases where archaeological evidence predominates, Bosch Gimpera's *Two Celtic Waves in Spain* plotted on the physical map the cultural range and composite heritage of pre-Roman and pre-Punic Celtiberia, and Randall MacIver's *Villanovans and Etruscans* delimited similar processes in Italy, emphasizing unawares the significance of primitive Rome, which has no counterpart in Iberia. Teuton and Slav illustrate, later, many aspects of those prehistoric movements; but the lands into which they came, like those occupied by the Galatian Celts, and by Hebrews and Arabs farther east, were already full of 'fenced cities', the debris of earlier regimes; and many of these survived as bazaar-cities or as sanctuaries. The tribal organization of these immigrants, their superimposed vassalage, and the 'frontier' outlook of them all, made their intrusions catastrophic, but brought elements, disruptive themselves, into regions where, as in the Mountain-zones of the New World, physical discontinuity gave to frontiersmen the utmost play, and checked the creation and maintenance of large 'rules of force'. Though there was much devastation, old inhabitants survived in most districts, to perpetuate contrasts of outlook and morale. The general acceptance of Christianity by the newcomers is sufficient evidence; that separation between town and country, which had worked so disastrously before, now provided the older population and higher culture, as in Bactria, with refuges and rallying points; and the mediaeval churches made full use of this vantage-ground, while the conquerors' demand for promised luxuries, and the opening of new markets for these in the barbarian north, gave to the bazaar-cities the same opportunity as to the sanctuaries. Their prestige, wealth, and municipal heritage thus made the mediaeval cities a means of 'maintaining life', and something more, in the mediaeval anarchy, but also an alternative to the larger loyalty essential to a nation-state, or even a territorial kingdom. The comparative failure of parliamentary institutions in Spain, Italy, and the Balkan lands is (in part at least) a heritage from those local loyalties, feudal and urban alike; and dynastic rule has hitherto been a frequent alternative.

All ancient cultures had their spiritual aspect, usually close-linked with their outlook on the material world, and on other men. Of some, there is the less need to speak here; for nature-worship in early Italy is the text of *The Golden Bough*, in the Near East, of *Adonis, Attis, and Osiris*, and *The Folklore of the Old Testament*.

In the Near East, it may be more than accident that all the greater immigrants wielded the spiritual weapon of a religion, newly tempered by a great mind; so that conquest was reinforced by proselytism. But the antecedents and effects of each were different. The Persians, like the northern immigrants, emerged from a long parkland discipline, but came, not to settle, nor primarily to plunder, but to rule—to leave this 'paradise' better than they found it. Hebrews and Arabs came out of nomadism, without that discipline, and the Turks with little of it; but the Hebrews, like the northern peoples, came seeking a 'promised land', and the Turks also to settle; the Arabs explicitly to plunder, and the Mongols to destroy all that interfered with pastoralism; but they, like the Turks, were Moslems when they reached the Mediterranean.

The Hebrew migration was on a small scale, and barely reached the sea; its widest sway was bounded by the Euphrates. But it was resumed in a 'dispersal' without parallel. Resistant to other cultures though all the 'dispersed' had been, the *Sephardim* nevertheless are distinguished from the rest by their long sojourn in Mediterranean lands. In Roman Africa the Jews seem to have been the cover under which old Punic enterprises persisted; in Cyrene they nearly created another Palestine; in Spain they preceded and outlasted Arab rule. Jerusalem, an early conquest, was a 'holy place' already, and became a sanctuary for two later religions. For a 'National Home' it is inevitably the capital. But it may be that the 'Dispersal' is the greater gift to mankind; the demonstration that congregationally men may colonize and trade where they will, interpenetrating other such 'dispersals'. There is only one risk, as on the high seas; the synagogue may 'spoil the Egyptians'.

The Achaemenid dynasty of Persia was the only ancient 'rule of force' that held any large part of the Mediterranean shores; for the kings of Sardis never ruled more than the western provinces of what had been the Hittite empire and then the Phrygian. The Persians differed also from all older theocracies, in their political philosophy, the Zoroastrian conception of a Lord of all Good, in truceless conflict with the Lord of Evil, certain to win in the end, but only quite certain to win, because all good things serve his purpose, and *if* all men of good will co-operate freely with him. His first minister on earth, Cyrus, 'the Servant of the Good Lord', required similar co-operation, and from all but the Greeks he won it and was 'king of kings'. Why he failed with the Greeks— and there were many who 'medized'—while he succeeded with the Jews, is a moral not an economic question. Had Darius continued his advance into Europe, even without Greek help, he would have anticipated much that the Ottoman Turk did later; and it was Persian conciliation of regional cultures, and of bazaars and sanctuaries—Sardis, Tyre and Jerusalem are examples— that was the foundation of Alexander's personal rule, of Seleucid and Pergamene administration, and of the provincial system of Rome and Byzantium. Of Zoroastrian contribution to later Judaism, to Christianity, and to Islam, it is enough to note that its significance begins to be recognized. 'Other sheep I have, that are not of this fold; them also I must bring' reads like a rescript of the 'Servant of the Good Lord', and became the message of Mithra, from Syria to the Tyne.

Christianity, propagated at first within Jewish synagogues, soon founded its own, becoming universal as well as personal. It brought the sanctuary to the votary, 'where two or three are gathered together'; but, like Judaism and Mithra-worship, it was congregational, and its congregations formed an empire-wide society. It was thus mainly urban, and did little to reconcile townsmen with *pagani*, who worshipped the 'little gods' long after the cities forsook the Olympians and *Sol Invictus*. Recognition by the civil power gave metropolitan Churches authority over conduct as well as belief, either in Byzantine accord with the State or in Western independence of it. Rome in particular became a sanctuary-city, but there were many little Romes, and the 'little gods' were converted along with their votaries, and as incompletely. In a great cathedral, as in Heaven, there are 'many mansions'. Insisting on the dignity and value of the individual, Christianity restrained traditional inhumanities, and devoted sanctuary wealth to relieve suffering and want. But fascinated by its own mysteries, like Greek philosophy, it ceased to 'consider the lilies'; directing men's attention to eternity, it relaxed their control of the present. While its 'kingdom is not of this world', it dominated the *orbis terrarum* for three centuries, and was evicted within another century from one half of it, Carthage failing to rank even with Alexandria and Antioch. That failure, against Vandal and Arab, to preserve the unity of the *orbis terrarum*, hard-won against Carthage and Cleopatra, opens the phase of Mediterranean culture in which we live.

Islam, another intensely personal religion, overwhelmed by consciousness of the Will of God, has (apart from a few ritual prescriptions) very elementary notions, *what it is* that God wills, and, since in Sunni belief Mohammed's revelation is the last, it therefore accepts fanatically one dynasty of his 'successors' after another, without outgrowing the desert-raider's reliance on 'holy war' to supply the needs of the 'faithful'. The consequent devastation of the country-side, where the pastoral has ever the advantage over the peasant, the caravan skill of the Arabs themselves, and their religious ardour, restored to bazaars and sanctuaries their pristine importance; nevertheless, it is in Moslem Africa that the most interesting relics survive of the primary economy. Confronted with two 'religions of the book', western Islam canonized the *Koran* and precluded the growth of doctrine which eastern, confronted with Mazdaism, admitted, at least in principle. The transference of the Caliphate from Damascus to Baghdad orientalized its antipathy to Hellenism, but in due time set Africa free on a course of its own. But that schism was the opportunity of the Ottoman Caliphate, which, so far as its influence extended, paralysed Arab culture for four centuries, and emphasized the schism of Sunni and Shia.

Both Seljuk and Ottoman Turks originated much farther away than the Persians, and in a wholly pastoral regime, but—unlike the Mongols, whose inroads were almost instantaneous, both of them, and especially the Seljuks, had had varied adventures within the Iranian section of the Mountain-zone before they entered Anatolia. Sivas and Konya—even Brusa—might be cities of Irak or Iran, and Tabriz or Isfahan Anatolian. Here literally, one may say, 'the route creates the social type'. The Ottoman Turk arrived more rapidly and less assimilated; and found so much prepared for him by the Seljuk 'Sultans of Rum', that he had less need to alter his own mode of life. With pastoral experience, he knew when to let flocks graze, and how to divide sheep from goats, so that he himself need not interfere. He accepted the major differences—which were by this time religious— among these human cattle as a principle both of devolution and of mutual dislike. It was only one step further, to kill off, or drive off, unprofitable herds, keeping those which gave least trouble or most produce. But the Ottoman estate remained a Mediterranean region; and its elements are familiar. Its primary economic groups are agricultural, with unabsorbed nomads here and there; bazaar-cities and caravan terminals have become railway junctions and ports; sanctuaries are turned into colleges. What was not new in 1453, and is new since 1923, is the political superstructure; the 'palace' of a personal monarch has been replaced by a technocracy; at its head is a President elected by the People's representatives; below, with responsible local self-government, are the same sturdy peasantry, industrious artisans, and hard-headed merchants as in the days of Croesus. They have social fraternity in Islam, political equality in the Republic, economic liberty already at least from foreign creditors. And this is the only Mediterranean state which has won through yet.

On its former subjects, Ottoman rule conferred quite unawares one notable benefit. There is some evidence for the view that, after profound disorganization of culture, and intermixture of physical breeds, a period of seclusion and quiescence is followed by fresh output of human energy and will, with a fresh outlook and fresh array of physical types to give effect to it. Certainly such a period of regeneration was enforced, however uneasily, by Ottoman rule, after a long period of northern immigration into Balkan lands; and to this Balkan renaissance, as we may well call it, coherent and intelligible pattern was given by Ottoman recognition of languages and religions as criteria; making Balkan nationalism, like Turkish nationalism itself, what it is. Among Moslem peoples also, outside Anatolia, the collapse of Ottoman rule has released what seems to be a renaissance, from Syria and Iraq to Morocco. Whether it is to be Arab and nationalist, or Pan-islamic and international, 'the coming days are the surest witness'.

One last point, to bring the long story up to date. We began our survey of Mediterranean advancement with geographical analysis of irrigation and navigation. Let us end with another geographical achievement. Hitherto the Mediterranean has been poor in mechanical power. So long as other regions also were power-less, that was no hardship. But in our time, mechanised power has been found and applied on an immense scale, with profound social results. Here, the sea is almost tideless, the steadier winds are seasonal, the forests have been consumed, coal is scarce and poor, oil still to be discovered. Hence, in the past, the prevalence of slavery, the persistence of home industries, the recent dependence on mass-produced goods from abroad. But the redistribution of highland water harnessed in its seaward descent to yield electric current, gives to Mediterranean lands their own reservoirs of power, and this power may be distributed to craftsmen in village homes; one of the greatest revolutions in their long history.

Epilogue

Let me summarize now, very briefly. Under Mediterranean conditions civilizable man spread, and still maintains himself, in small almost self-sufficient economic groups, essentially engaged in a multiple food-quest—corn, wine and oil—to which flocks and herds are subsidiary. Material amenities are supplied through bazaar-cities, needs of the soul through sanctuaries, needs of the exceptional or superfluous man by adventure. These primary communities were brought into a single maritime association through navigation, which also offered relief from over-crowding, and assisted the propagation of a few highly specialized types of society—Greek, Phoenician, Etruscan—which all failed to assimilate the primary economies among which they came. Sea-power abused became piracy, parasitic, endemic, and very difficult to suppress. Intruders from without have been essentially *either* transformed by transit through the Mountain-zone, *or* uncivilized nomads emerging directly from the grassland, and impelled by religious enthusiasms which neither Roman administration nor Christian doctrine were able to expel from about one half of the 'ring of lands'. Wherever lands thus disorganized remain inhabited, the primary economic groups persist or reappear. It is inferred that all political superstructures depend for their vitality on these economic foundations.

In this summary analysis—which, if not quite historical geography, is offered as an essay in geographical history— I have tried to present main features of an exceptional human habitat and its primary economy, the chief devices of man which have brought its shores together, and the undesigned contributions of intruders and aggressors; and to illustrate thereby some phases of its culture. Like some of its typical regions—Crete, Sicily, Rhodes, and Cyprus— the Mediterranean has had great moments, when it seemed to hold in its sway the future of mankind; and crises of devastation, from which recovery seemed beyond hope. But short of a planetary convulsion, there will always be a Mediterranean, with characteristic mode of life and outlook. Its peoples and states rise and fall; the momentary master of its fate is 'he who slays the slayer, and shall himself be slain'; but the prize of victory remains, and like its own miracle, the Golden Bough, it restores its vitality: *uno avulso, non deficit alter aureus.*